The Power of Documentary: Understanding the Impact of Non-Fiction Media on Students

Anders Leroy

Copyright © [2023]

Title: The Power of Documentary: Understanding the Impact of Non-Fiction Media on Students

Author's: Anders Leroy

This book was printed and published by [Publisher's: **Anders Leroy**] in [2023]

ISBN:

TABLE OF CONTENT

Chapter 3: Documentaries as Tools for Social Awareness and Activism 33

Chapter 4: Documentary Ethics and Media Literacy 45

Chapter 5: Integrating Documentaries into the Classroom   57

Chapter 6: The Future of Documentary Education   70

Chapter 1: Introduction to the Power of Documentary

The Importance of Non-Fiction Media in Education

In this digital age, where information is just a click away, non-fiction media has emerged as a powerful tool in education. From documentaries to news articles, this non-fiction content provides students with a deeper understanding of the world around them. As students pursuing film and media studies, it is essential to recognize the significance of non-fiction media in shaping our education and broadening our perspectives.

Firstly, non-fiction media offers a tangible connection between theory and practice. While textbooks and lectures provide valuable knowledge, non-fiction media brings subjects to life by showcasing real-life examples and events. By watching documentaries or analyzing news reports, students can witness firsthand how concepts and theories apply to real-world scenarios. This engagement fosters critical thinking skills, enabling students to analyze, evaluate, and form their own opinions on the subjects being presented.

Moreover, non-fiction media has the power to inspire and evoke empathy. Documentaries, in particular, offer us a window into diverse cultures, historical events, and social issues. By immersing ourselves in these stories, we gain a deeper understanding of the human experience and develop empathy towards different perspectives. This empathy is crucial for film and media students, as it allows us to create impactful content that resonates with audiences on a global scale.

Furthermore, non-fiction media promotes media literacy and information literacy. In an era of fake news and misinformation, it is vital for students to develop critical media consumption skills. Non-fiction media serves as a platform to explore different sources, evaluate credibility, and fact-check information. By engaging with non-fiction media, students learn to discern between reliable and unreliable sources, thus becoming more informed and responsible media consumers.

Lastly, non-fiction media sparks curiosity and encourages lifelong learning. Through documentaries and news articles, students discover new topics, cultures, and ideas that they may not have encountered otherwise. This exposure to diverse content broadens their horizons and motivates them to delve deeper into subjects that pique their interest. Non-fiction media acts as a catalyst for intellectual growth, inspiring students to continue their education beyond the classroom.

In conclusion, non-fiction media plays a pivotal role in education, particularly for students pursuing film and media studies. It bridges the gap between theory and practice, fosters critical thinking and empathy, promotes media and information literacy, and ignites curiosity for lifelong learning. As students, embracing non-fiction media will enhance our education and equip us with the skills necessary to navigate the complexities of the media landscape. Let us recognize the power of non-fiction media and harness its potential to become informed, responsible, and impactful professionals in the field of film and media studies.

The Role of Documentaries in Expanding Students' Perspectives

In today's digital age, where information is readily available at our fingertips, documentaries have emerged as a powerful tool for expanding students' perspectives. The world of film and media studies has witnessed a significant shift towards embracing documentaries as a means of education and enlightenment. These non-fiction films offer a unique and immersive experience that goes beyond the traditional classroom setting, allowing students to explore a multitude of topics and gain a deeper understanding of the world around them.

One of the most significant roles documentaries play in expanding students' perspectives is by shedding light on diverse and often marginalized voices. Through these films, students are exposed to narratives and experiences that they may not encounter in their everyday lives. Documentaries have the power to challenge preconceived notions and biases, fostering empathy and understanding among students. Whether it's exploring the struggles of individuals from different cultural backgrounds, examining social justice issues, or shedding light on environmental concerns, documentaries provide a platform for underrepresented voices to be heard.

Furthermore, documentaries offer an alternative mode of storytelling that engages students in a way that traditional textbooks cannot. The visual and auditory elements of documentaries create a multisensory experience, making the content more memorable and impactful. Students are not only learning facts and figures but also experiencing emotions and connecting with the subjects of the film. This immersive experience helps students develop critical thinking skills as they analyze and interpret the information presented in the documentary.

Documentaries also provide an opportunity for students to develop media literacy skills. In an era of fake news and misinformation, it is crucial for students to be able to discern between reliable sources and propaganda. Documentaries, when carefully selected, can serve as a reliable source of information, presenting well-researched and well-documented content. By critically analyzing the techniques used in documentaries, students can learn to evaluate the credibility and bias of media sources, equipping them with the skills necessary to navigate the media landscape.

In conclusion, documentaries have become an invaluable resource for students studying film and media studies. These non-fiction films have the power to expand students' perspectives by introducing them to diverse voices, fostering empathy, and developing critical thinking skills. Through documentaries, students can explore a wide range of topics and gain a deeper understanding of the world around them. As the digital age continues to evolve, the role of documentaries in education will only become more significant, empowering students to become engaged and informed global citizens.

Benefits of Documentary Viewing for Student Learning

Introduction:
In the era of multimedia, documentaries have emerged as powerful tools for learning and understanding the world around us. By presenting real-life stories, facts, and perspectives, documentaries offer a unique learning experience that engages students in ways traditional textbooks may not. This subchapter will explore the numerous benefits of documentary viewing for student learning, particularly for students in the niche fields of film and media studies.

1. Visual and Engaging Learning:
Documentaries bring subjects to life by providing visual and auditory stimuli that captivate students' attention. Through the use of compelling storytelling techniques, stunning visuals, and real-life interviews, documentaries create an immersive learning environment that enhances student engagement. By witnessing real people and events, students can better grasp complex concepts and develop a deeper understanding of the subject matter.

2. Multidisciplinary Learning:
Documentaries often cover a wide range of topics, from history to science, culture to politics. This multidisciplinary approach enables students to explore various subjects and make connections between different fields of study. By exposing students to diverse perspectives, documentaries foster critical thinking and the ability to analyze and synthesize information from multiple sources.

3. Cultural Awareness and Empathy:
Documentaries provide a window into different cultures, introducing

students to the realities and challenges faced by individuals worldwide. Through exposure to different social, economic, and political contexts, students can develop empathy, cross-cultural understanding, and a global perspective. This enhanced cultural awareness is particularly valuable for students in film and media studies, as it broadens their ability to create meaningful and inclusive media content.

4.   Authentic   Learning   Experiences: Documentaries offer an authentic and unfiltered portrayal of real-life situations, allowing students to witness events as they unfold. This authenticity provides students with firsthand experiences and exposes them to diverse viewpoints, challenging their preconceived notions and encouraging critical thinking. By analyzing and discussing the content of documentaries, students can develop their communication skills and engage in meaningful dialogue.

5.   Inspirational   and   Motivational: Documentaries often showcase individuals who have overcome adversity, achieved great success, or made a significant impact on society. By presenting these real-life stories, documentaries can inspire and motivate students to pursue their passions and make a difference in the world. These stories of resilience, creativity, and innovation can serve as powerful role models for students in film and media studies, encouraging them to explore new avenues and push the boundaries of their own creativity.

Conclusion:
Documentaries have the potential to revolutionize student learning by offering a dynamic and immersive educational experience. Through their visual appeal, interdisciplinary approach, cultural awareness,

authenticity, and inspiring narratives, documentaries provide students in film and media studies with unique opportunities for growth and learning. By incorporating documentaries into their educational journey, students can expand their knowledge, enhance their critical thinking skills, and become more empathetic and culturally aware individuals.

Understanding the Influence of Documentary on Students' Perception

In the realm of film and media studies, documentaries hold a unique place as powerful tools for educating, informing, and shaping our perception of the world. Documentaries have the ability to capture reality in a way that no other medium can, allowing audiences to gain a deeper understanding of diverse subjects and issues. In this subchapter, we will explore how documentaries influence students' perception and why they should be an integral part of any film and media studies curriculum.

First and foremost, documentaries offer an authentic and unfiltered view of the world. Unlike fictional films, documentaries present real people, real events, and real stories. This authenticity allows students to connect with the subject matter on a more personal level, fostering empathy and a deeper understanding of diverse cultures, social issues, and global challenges. By exposing students to different perspectives and experiences, documentaries broaden their horizons and encourage critical thinking.

Furthermore, documentaries possess the power to challenge preconceived notions and biases. They shed light on underrepresented voices and marginalized communities, bringing attention to social injustices and systemic problems. By confronting students with uncomfortable truths, documentaries encourage them to question their own beliefs and assumptions, fostering a more open-minded and inclusive worldview.

Documentaries also play a vital role in promoting media literacy among students. In an era of fake news and misinformation, it is crucial for students to develop critical thinking skills and the ability to distinguish between reliable sources and propaganda. Documentaries, with their emphasis on research, evidence, and expert analysis, provide students with valuable tools to navigate the complex media landscape.

Moreover, documentaries have the potential to inspire and empower students to become agents of change. By showcasing real-life stories of resilience, activism, and social transformation, documentaries instill a sense of agency and encourage students to take action. They demonstrate that even the smallest individual actions can make a significant difference in the world.

In conclusion, understanding the influence of documentaries on students' perception is essential for any student studying film and media. Documentaries have the power to educate, challenge, and inspire, fostering empathy, critical thinking, and a commitment to social change. By embracing documentaries as a valuable educational resource, students can develop a more nuanced understanding of the world and become active contributors to a more just and equitable society.

The Psychological Impact of Non-Fiction Media

In the realm of film and media studies, non-fiction media, particularly documentaries, hold a unique power to shape our perceptions, challenge our beliefs, and evoke emotional responses. These forms of media have the ability to transport us to different worlds, expose us to new ideas, and shed light on pressing social issues. However, it is important to recognize that their impact on our psyche goes beyond simple entertainment or education. Non-fiction media can have a profound psychological impact on students, influencing their thoughts, emotions, and even behavior.

One of the key psychological impacts of non-fiction media is its ability to create empathy. Documentaries often depict real-life stories that resonate with viewers, triggering an emotional response and fostering a sense of connection with the subjects portrayed. This emotional engagement can lead to increased empathy and understanding towards individuals from different backgrounds or experiencing adversity. By witnessing the struggles and triumphs of others, students can develop a greater sense of compassion and an expanded worldview.

Moreover, non-fiction media can also shape our beliefs and attitudes. Documentaries have the power to challenge preconceived notions and present alternative perspectives on various topics. By presenting compelling evidence and thought-provoking arguments, non-fiction media can influence students' opinions and encourage critical thinking. It prompts us to question our own biases and reevaluate our positions, fostering intellectual growth and a deeper understanding of complex issues.

However, it is crucial to acknowledge that non-fiction media can also have negative psychological impacts. Certain documentaries may contain distressing content, such as graphic violence or traumatic events. Exposure to such material can lead to feelings of sadness, anxiety, or even secondary trauma. It is vital for students to engage with non-fiction media in a responsible and mindful manner, being aware of their emotional limits and seeking support when needed.

To harness the psychological impact of non-fiction media effectively, students should approach these forms of media with a critical and discerning eye. They should actively engage with the content, questioning its authenticity, biases, and potential impact. By doing so, students can develop media literacy skills, enabling them to navigate the complex world of non-fiction media and make informed judgments.

In conclusion, the psychological impact of non-fiction media on students, particularly in the realm of film and media studies, is significant. These forms of media have the power to shape empathy, influence beliefs, and prompt critical thinking. However, it is crucial for students to approach non-fiction media with caution, being mindful of its potential negative impacts and practicing media literacy. By understanding the psychological effects of non-fiction media, students can harness its power to foster personal growth, social awareness, and intellectual development.

How Documentaries Shape Students' Worldviews

In today's digital age, documentaries have become a powerful and influential medium that has the ability to shape and transform our understanding of the world. As students, especially those studying film and media studies, it is important to recognize and appreciate the impact that documentaries can have on our worldview.

Documentaries are not mere entertainment; they provide us with a unique perspective on various subjects, shedding light on important issues and challenging our preconceived notions. Through thought-provoking narratives, interviews with experts, and compelling visuals, documentaries have the power to educate, inform, and inspire change.

One of the ways documentaries shape students' worldviews is by exposing them to diverse perspectives. These films often explore topics that are not commonly discussed in mainstream media, giving students a deeper understanding of different cultures, social issues, and global events. By presenting multiple viewpoints, documentaries encourage critical thinking and help students develop a more nuanced understanding of complex topics.

Furthermore, documentaries can evoke empathy and compassion within students. By bringing real stories and real people to the forefront, these films can elicit emotional responses and encourage students to connect with the experiences of others. This emotional engagement can lead to increased awareness and a motivation to take action, whether it be through volunteer work, advocacy, or simply spreading awareness.

Moreover, documentaries provide an opportunity for students to analyze and deconstruct the techniques used in non-fiction media. By studying the structure, editing, and storytelling methods employed in documentaries, students can gain valuable insights into the art of filmmaking and storytelling. This knowledge can be applied to their own work, allowing them to create impactful and meaningful films in the future.

However, it is important to approach documentaries with a critical eye. While these films can be powerful tools for shaping our worldviews, they are not immune to bias or manipulation. Students should always question the sources, motives, and perspectives presented in documentaries, ensuring a well-rounded understanding of the subject matter.

In conclusion, documentaries have the potential to shape students' worldviews by exposing them to diverse perspectives, evoking empathy, and providing an opportunity for critical analysis. As students studying film and media studies, it is crucial to explore and appreciate the power of documentaries in order to become informed, empathetic, and socially conscious individuals.

Chapter 2: The Role of Documentary in Critical Thinking

Developing Analytical Skills through Documentary Analysis

In the realm of film and media studies, documentaries hold a unique position. They not only entertain and inform but also have the power to shape our understanding of the world. As students diving into this field, it is crucial to develop strong analytical skills that will enable us to critically evaluate and appreciate the impact of non-fiction media, such as documentaries.

This subchapter aims to highlight the significance of documentary analysis in honing our analytical skills. By exploring various aspects of documentary filmmaking, we can garner a deeper understanding of the techniques employed by filmmakers to convey their messages effectively.

One fundamental aspect of documentary analysis involves examining the filmmaker's intention and point of view. Documentaries often present a specific perspective on a subject, and it is crucial for students to question and evaluate the biases or motivations behind these choices. By doing so, we can develop a more discerning eye and avoid passively absorbing information without critical thought.

Another essential skill to develop is the ability to identify and analyze the documentary's structure and narrative techniques. Documentaries are crafted with a purpose, and understanding the techniques employed in storytelling can help us comprehend the intended impact on the audience. By dissecting the use of interviews, archival footage, voice-overs, and music, we can recognize the nuances and strategies employed to engage viewers and evoke emotional responses.

Furthermore, documentary analysis encourages us to consider the socio-political implications of the subject matter. Documentaries often tackle issues that influence society, and by critically examining the way these topics are presented, we can gain insights into the broader implications and consequences. This skill is essential for understanding the power of documentaries in shaping public opinion and initiating social change.

Lastly, documentary analysis provides an excellent opportunity for interdisciplinary study. By exploring the intersections between film and media studies and other fields such as sociology, psychology, or history, we can develop a more holistic understanding of the subject matter. Analyzing documentaries from multiple perspectives enhances our critical thinking abilities and encourages us to challenge preconceived notions.

In conclusion, developing analytical skills through documentary analysis is essential for students in the field of film and media studies. By critically evaluating the intentions, structure, and socio-political implications of documentaries, we can become more informed and discerning viewers. This skill set not only enhances our understanding of non-fiction media but also equips us to analyze and engage with the world around us more effectively.

Engaging with Different Perspectives in Documentaries

In today's world, documentaries have become an important form of media that not only entertain but also educate and inspire. As students in the field of film and media studies, it is crucial to understand the power of documentaries in shaping public opinion and providing a platform for diverse perspectives. This subchapter explores the significance of engaging with different perspectives in documentaries and how it contributes to our understanding of the world around us.

Documentaries are unique in their ability to present real-life stories, issues, and events. They offer a glimpse into the lives of people from different walks of life, cultures, and socio-economic backgrounds. By engaging with documentaries that present diverse perspectives, students can develop a broader understanding and empathy for individuals whose experiences may differ from their own.

One of the key benefits of engaging with different perspectives in documentaries is the opportunity to challenge our own biases and preconceived notions. As students, it is essential to approach documentaries with an open mind, ready to question our own beliefs and opinions. By actively seeking out documentaries that present different viewpoints, we can expand our worldview and develop critical thinking skills.

Furthermore, engaging with different perspectives in documentaries allows us to gain a more comprehensive understanding of complex social issues. Documentaries often shed light on topics that are marginalized or underrepresented in mainstream media. By exploring these perspectives, we can uncover the structural inequalities and systemic problems that exist in our society. This knowledge empowers students to become agents of change and advocates for social justice.

Engagement with different perspectives in documentaries also fosters cultural competency and intercultural understanding. By exposing ourselves to diverse stories and experiences, we can break down barriers and bridge the gaps between different communities. This understanding is crucial in a globalized world where cultural exchange and collaboration are becoming increasingly important.

In conclusion, the power of documentaries lies in their ability to provide a platform for different perspectives. Engaging with documentaries that present diverse viewpoints allows students in the field of film and media studies to challenge their own biases, gain a comprehensive understanding of social issues, and foster intercultural understanding. By embracing these different perspectives, students can become informed and responsible media consumers who are capable of making a positive impact on society.

Identifying Bias and Manipulation in Non-Fiction Media

Subchapter: Identifying Bias and Manipulation in Non-Fiction Media

Introduction:

In the world of non-fiction media, it is crucial for students studying film and media studies to develop a critical eye when it comes to identifying bias and manipulation. This subchapter aims to equip you, as students, with the tools and knowledge needed to navigate the complex landscape of non-fiction media and understand its impact. By recognizing bias and manipulation, you can become more discerning viewers and consumers of information.

Understanding Bias:

Bias refers to the inclination or prejudice in favor of or against a particular viewpoint, person, or group. It can manifest in various forms such as political, cultural, or personal biases. Recognizing bias is the first step towards analyzing non-fiction media accurately. To identify bias, consider the following:

1. Source Evaluation: Analyze the credibility and reputation of the source. Is it known for its objectivity or does it have a clear agenda?

2. Language and Tone: Pay attention to the language used in the media. Is it neutral or loaded with emotions? Does the tone seem balanced or one-sided?

3. Omission and Selection: Examine what information is included and what is left out. Are certain perspectives or facts deliberately excluded to strengthen a particular bias?

Detecting Manipulation:

Manipulation in non-fiction media involves intentionally distorting facts or employing persuasive techniques to sway the audience's opinions. To identify manipulation, keep the following in mind:

1. Emotional Appeals: Look out for excessive use of emotional content that aims to evoke a specific response rather than presenting a rational argument.

2. Visual Techniques: Pay attention to the use of camera angles, editing, and music. These elements can create a specific atmosphere or manipulate the audience's emotions.

3. Cherry-picking Evidence: Analyze whether the media selectively presents evidence or only highlights information that supports a specific narrative while ignoring contradictory facts.

Developing a Critical Eye:

To become discerning viewers of non-fiction media, it is essential to approach each piece of content with a critical mindset. Consider the following strategies:

1. Cross-referencing: Verify information by consulting multiple sources to gain a broader perspective and ensure accuracy.

2. Fact-checking: Utilize fact-checking websites and resources to verify claims and debunk misinformation.

3. Engage in Dialogue: Discuss the media content with peers, instructors, or experts to gain different perspectives and challenge your own biases.

Conclusion:

Being able to identify bias and manipulation in non-fiction media is a crucial skill for students studying film and media studies. By understanding and recognizing these techniques, you can become more informed and critical consumers of information. Developing a discerning eye will not only enhance your academic pursuits but also empower you to engage with the media in a more thoughtful and responsible manner.

Enhancing Research and Fact-Checking Skills through Documentary Studies

In today's digital age, where information is easily accessible but often accompanied by misinformation and fake news, the ability to research and fact-check has become more crucial than ever. As students of film and media studies, you have a unique advantage in developing these skills through documentary studies. By immersing yourself in the world of non-fiction media, you can enhance your research abilities, sharpen your critical thinking, and become more discerning consumers of information.

Documentary studies offer a wealth of opportunities to explore diverse topics and subjects. Whether it's a historical event, social issue, or even an individual's life story, documentaries provide an in-depth look at real-life situations and the people involved. As students, this allows you to tap into a vast array of primary sources, including interviews, archival footage, and expert opinions, which can serve as valuable research material.

To make the most of your documentary studies, it is important to adopt a systematic approach to research. Start by identifying your research question or topic of interest. This will help you narrow down your focus and guide your exploration. Once you have a clear direction, dive into the world of documentaries. Watch films that align with your research question, take notes, and pay attention to the sources and evidence presented. Be critical of the information presented and cross-reference it with other reliable sources to ensure accuracy and credibility.

Documentary studies also offer an opportunity to develop fact-checking skills. As you engage with various documentaries, be vigilant about verifying the information presented. Look for corroborating evidence from other reliable sources, consult scholarly articles and books, and consider different perspectives on the topic. Fact-checking not only enhances your research skills but also equips you with the ability to differentiate between reliable information and misinformation.

Moreover, engaging with documentaries encourages critical thinking. As you analyze the filmmaker's perspective and storytelling techniques, you develop a more discerning eye. You learn to critically evaluate the credibility of the sources, consider the biases and motivations behind the storytelling, and question the underlying assumptions. This critical thinking mindset will empower you to approach all forms of media with a skeptical eye, helping you become more informed and responsible consumers of information.

In conclusion, documentary studies provide an excellent platform for enhancing your research and fact-checking skills. By immersing yourself in non-fiction media, you can access a wealth of primary sources, develop fact-checking abilities, and cultivate critical thinking skills. These skills are not only valuable for your academic pursuits but also essential for navigating the complex world of media and information. So, dive into the world of documentaries, engage with diverse perspectives, and empower yourself as a well-informed and critical thinker.

Utilizing Documentaries as Primary Sources for Research

In today's digital age, where information is readily accessible, students must critically evaluate sources to ensure the credibility and reliability of their research. While books, scholarly articles, and academic journals remain popular choices, documentaries offer a unique and valuable perspective as primary sources for research, especially in the field of film and media studies. The power of documentaries lies in their ability to combine the art of storytelling with factual information, providing a captivating and informative medium for students to explore and analyze.

One of the main advantages of using documentaries as primary sources is their ability to bring real-life experiences and events to the forefront. By watching a documentary, students can gain insights into various topics, such as historical events, social issues, or cultural phenomena, that might otherwise be difficult to comprehend through traditional research materials. Documentaries capture the essence of these subjects through interviews, firsthand accounts, and visual evidence, allowing students to form a deeper understanding and connection with the topic they are studying.

Furthermore, documentaries often present multiple perspectives and voices, making them valuable tools for critical thinking and analysis. As students delve into a documentary, they are exposed to different viewpoints, ideologies, and arguments. This exposure encourages them to question, evaluate, and form their own opinions based on an array of perspectives. By utilizing documentaries as primary sources, students can develop their analytical and critical thinking abilities, enabling them to engage in informed discussions and make well-rounded arguments in their research papers.

Documentaries also offer a dynamic and engaging approach to learning. Rather than solely relying on text-based research materials, students can immerse themselves in the audio-visual world of documentaries. This medium stimulates both visual and auditory senses, making the learning experience more memorable and enjoyable. The power of storytelling in documentaries can evoke emotions, challenge preconceived notions, and inspire students to further explore the subject matter.

As with any primary source, it is crucial for students to critically evaluate documentaries for accuracy, bias, and credibility. They should consider the credentials of filmmakers, fact-check the information presented, and compare it with other reliable sources. By doing so, students can effectively utilize documentaries as primary sources for research while maintaining academic integrity.

In conclusion, documentaries are valuable primary sources that students in the field of film and media studies can utilize to enhance their research. Documentaries offer a unique blend of storytelling, factual information, and diverse perspectives, allowing students to gain a deeper understanding of their subject matter. By critically evaluating documentaries and incorporating them into their research, students can develop critical thinking skills, engage in informed discussions, and create well-rounded arguments in their academic work.

Verifying Information and Fact-Checking in Documentaries

In the world of film and media studies, documentaries hold a unique power to educate, inspire, and challenge our perspectives. As students exploring the impact of non-fiction media, it is crucial to understand the importance of verifying information and fact-checking in documentaries. While these films aim to shed light on real-world issues and present a truthful narrative, it is essential to critically examine the information presented and ensure its accuracy.

Documentaries are often considered a reliable source of information, with their objective being to inform and educate viewers about various subjects. However, filmmakers can sometimes inadvertently present biased or misleading information, whether intentional or not. As students, it falls upon us to critically analyze the content and verify the facts presented before accepting them as truth.

To begin with, one must understand the various techniques and methods employed in documentary filmmaking. Filmmakers use interviews, archival footage, and expert opinions to build their narratives. While these sources may seem credible, it is important to cross-reference information with multiple sources to ensure accuracy. This process involves fact-checking claims, verifying statistics, and corroborating evidence through reliable and reputable sources.

Furthermore, it is essential to consider the perspective and agenda of the filmmaker. Just like any other form of media, documentaries can be influenced by biases, political motivations, or personal beliefs. By understanding the filmmaker's intentions and biases, we can better evaluate the information presented and identify any potential manipulation or distortion of facts.

In the digital age, where information spreads rapidly and can be easily manipulated, fact-checking becomes even more imperative. With the advent of social media and online platforms, misinformation can quickly infiltrate our screens. As students, we must utilize various fact-checking tools and resources available to us. Websites such as Snopes, FactCheck.org, and PolitiFact can help verify claims and debunk falsehoods.

Moreover, engaging in discussions and seeking out diverse perspectives can deepen our understanding of a particular issue. By actively participating in critical conversations and debates, we can challenge our own biases and gain a more nuanced understanding of complex topics.

In conclusion, verifying information and fact-checking in documentaries is crucial for students studying film and media studies. As viewers, it is our responsibility to critically analyze the content presented and ensure its accuracy by cross-referencing information, considering the filmmaker's perspective, and utilizing fact-checking tools. By doing so, we can separate truth from fiction and develop a more informed and critical approach to understanding the impact of non-fiction media.

Chapter 3: Documentaries as Tools for Social Awareness and Activism

Inspiring Empathy and Compassion through Documentary Narratives

Documentaries have the unique power to transport us into the lives of others, allowing us to experience their struggles, triumphs, and emotions firsthand. As students of film and media studies, we have the privilege of exploring the incredible impact that documentary narratives can have on inspiring empathy and compassion in our society.

Through the lens of a camera, documentary filmmakers capture real-life stories that are often overlooked or misunderstood. These narratives shed light on social issues, cultural differences, and personal journeys, providing us with a deeper understanding of the world we live in. By immersing ourselves in these stories, we can develop a sense of empathy and compassion for those who are different from us.

One of the key strengths of documentary narratives is their ability to portray diverse perspectives and challenge preconceived notions. As students, we have a responsibility to critically analyze these narratives and question our own biases. By doing so, we can expand our worldview and foster empathy towards people whose experiences may differ from our own. These documentaries can serve as powerful tools to bridge gaps between individuals and cultures, fostering understanding and compassion.

Moreover, documentary narratives have the potential to inspire action and social change. When we witness the struggles faced by individuals or communities through the lens of a documentary, we are motivated to make a difference. As students, we can use these narratives as catalysts for activism and advocacy, working towards a more inclusive and compassionate society.

In our studies, we should explore various documentary genres and techniques employed by filmmakers to evoke empathy and compassion. From personal testimonials to historical accounts, from observational documentaries to participatory approaches, each style has its own way of engaging the viewer emotionally. Understanding these techniques will not only enhance our appreciation for the art of documentary filmmaking but also enable us to create meaningful narratives that inspire empathy and compassion in others.

As students of film and media studies, we have the power to harness the potential of documentary narratives to foster empathy and compassion. By immersing ourselves in these stories, questioning our biases, and utilizing our skills to create impactful content, we can make a difference in the world. Let us embrace the power of documentary and use it as a tool to inspire empathy, understanding, and positive change in our society.

Understanding Different Cultures and Lifestyles through Documentaries

In today's globalized world, it is essential for students studying film and media studies to explore and understand different cultures and lifestyles. Documentaries, as a form of non-fiction media, have the power to transport viewers to different corners of the world, offering a unique window into the lives of people from diverse backgrounds. This subchapter delves into the significance of documentaries as a means to gain insight into various cultures and lifestyles.

Documentaries provide an immersive experience that allows students to witness the realities of different cultures firsthand. By capturing the lives of individuals, communities, and societies, documentaries enable students to comprehend the nuances of different cultures, traditions, and ways of life. Through vivid imagery, compelling narratives, and authentic voices, documentaries offer a deep understanding of the challenges, triumphs, and daily experiences of people from all walks of life.

Moreover, documentaries often shed light on social issues and provide a platform for marginalized communities to share their stories. By exposing students to the struggles faced by different cultures and lifestyles, documentaries can foster empathy and inspire a commitment to social justice. They break stereotypes and challenge preconceived notions, encouraging students to question their own biases and develop a broader worldview.

Documentaries also serve as powerful educational tools, allowing students to analyze and critically evaluate the content they consume.

By studying the techniques and methodologies employed by documentary filmmakers, students can learn about the art of storytelling and gain insights into the ethical considerations involved in representing different cultures and lifestyles. This subchapter will explore various documentary styles, such as observational, participatory, and reflexive, and their impact on audience engagement and understanding.

Furthermore, documentaries offer a platform for students to engage in meaningful discussions and debates about cultural diversity and social issues. By analyzing and interpreting different documentaries, students can develop their analytical and communication skills, while also enhancing their cultural competence. This subchapter will provide examples of documentaries that have successfully sparked conversations and brought about social change.

In conclusion, documentaries have the power to bridge gaps between cultures and lifestyles by offering a unique and authentic perspective into the lives of diverse individuals. By immersing themselves in the world of documentaries, students studying film and media studies can broaden their horizons, develop empathy, and acquire the tools necessary to critically engage with non-fiction media. Thus, understanding different cultures and lifestyles through documentaries is not only educational but also transformative, enabling students to become more informed and compassionate global citizens.

Fostering Understanding and Tolerance through Non-Fiction Media

In our increasingly diverse and interconnected world, it is crucial for students of film and media studies to recognize the power of non-fiction media in fostering understanding and tolerance. Documentaries, in particular, have the unique ability to shed light on various social, cultural, and political issues, offering a platform for marginalized voices and challenging preconceived notions. This subchapter explores how non-fiction media can be a catalyst for empathy, dialogue, and positive social change.

Non-fiction media, such as documentaries, offer an authentic representation of real-world experiences and perspectives. By immersing ourselves in these narratives, we gain a deeper understanding of different cultures, identities, and socio-political contexts. Documentaries have the potential to challenge stereotypes, debunk myths, and expose hidden truths, enabling students to critically analyze the complexities of our global society.

Through non-fiction media, students can explore topics such as race, gender, sexuality, immigration, and environmental issues, among others. By engaging with these narratives, students develop empathy and a sense of connection to the experiences of others. This empathy, in turn, fosters tolerance and compassion, as it allows students to see beyond their own perspectives and acknowledge the diverse realities that exist.

Furthermore, non-fiction media encourages dialogue and debate among students. By sharing their thoughts and engaging in respectful discussions, students can challenge their own biases and learn from one another's experiences. Documentaries often serve as a starting point for these conversations, providing a shared language and a framework for critical analysis. Through these discussions, students can develop their analytical skills and become active participants in shaping a more inclusive and just society.

Non-fiction media also has the power to inspire action. When students are exposed to the struggles and triumphs presented in documentaries, they are often motivated to make a difference. Whether it is through volunteering, advocacy, or pursuing careers in social justice, non-fiction media can ignite a passion for positive social change.

In conclusion, non-fiction media, particularly documentaries, can be a powerful tool in fostering understanding and tolerance among students of film and media studies. By exposing students to diverse narratives and perspectives, documentaries enable empathy, dialogue, and the potential for positive social change. As future filmmakers and media professionals, it is vital for students to recognize the impact they can have on shaping a more inclusive and equitable world through the power of non-fiction media.

Promoting Social Justice and Advocacy through Documentary Filmmaking

In the age of digital media and information overload, documentary filmmaking has emerged as a powerful tool for promoting social justice and advocacy. This subchapter aims to explore the profound impact of non-fiction media on students, particularly those studying film and media studies, and how they can leverage the power of documentary to bring about positive change in society.

Documentary filmmaking has the unique ability to shed light on important social issues, challenge prevailing narratives, and give voice to marginalized communities. By delving deep into real-life stories and experiences, documentaries have the power to evoke empathy, provoke thought, and inspire action among viewers. As students of film and media studies, it is crucial to recognize the potential of this medium as a catalyst for social change.

One of the key aspects of promoting social justice and advocacy through documentary filmmaking is choosing compelling and relevant subject matters. By selecting topics that address pressing social issues such as racial inequality, gender discrimination, environmental degradation, or poverty, students can create documentaries that not only educate but also motivate audiences to take action. Researching and understanding the context and background of the issue is essential in order to present a comprehensive and nuanced perspective.

Furthermore, documentary filmmakers must adopt ethical practices and maintain integrity in their storytelling. It is important to respect the dignity and privacy of individuals featured in the film, ensuring their voices are accurately represented and their stories are not exploited for personal gain. This can be achieved through thorough research, interviews, and collaboration with communities and individuals directly affected by the issue at hand.

To effectively promote social justice and advocacy, it is imperative to reach a wider audience. This can be achieved through film festivals, screenings, online platforms, and social media. Engaging with viewers through post-screening discussions, workshops, and educational initiatives can further amplify the impact of the documentary and encourage dialogue and action.

In conclusion, documentary filmmaking holds immense potential for students studying film and media studies to become agents of social change. By selecting relevant topics, adhering to ethical practices, and effectively disseminating their documentaries, students can contribute to promoting social justice and advocacy in a meaningful and impactful way. Through the power of non-fiction media, they can inspire empathy, challenge societal norms, and ultimately create a more inclusive and just society.

Documentaries as Catalysts for Change

Subchapter: Documentaries as Catalysts for Change

Introduction:
In today's rapidly evolving world, the power of documentaries as catalysts for change cannot be underestimated. Documentaries have the ability to inform, educate, and ignite a sense of social responsibility among viewers. In this subchapter, we will explore how documentaries have become pivotal in shaping public opinion, raising awareness, and inspiring action. As students of film and media studies, understanding the impact of non-fiction media is crucial to becoming informed citizens and effective storytellers.

Shaping   Public   Opinion:
Documentaries have the unique ability to present complex issues in a compelling and accessible manner. Through the use of interviews, archival footage, and expert commentary, filmmakers can bring attention to social, political, and environmental issues that may have otherwise remained hidden. By presenting multiple perspectives and fostering critical thinking, documentaries challenge preconceived notions, encouraging viewers to question the status quo and consider alternative viewpoints.

Raising   Awareness:
Documentaries provide a platform for marginalized voices and underrepresented communities. They shed light on social injustices, human rights violations, and environmental crises that demand attention. By bringing these issues to the forefront, documentaries create a sense of urgency and compel viewers to take action. As

students, we have the opportunity to amplify these voices, inspire empathy, and contribute to positive change by sharing these stories with a wider audience.

Inspiring Action:
Documentaries not only inform and raise awareness but also motivate viewers to take action. They provide a roadmap for activism, showcasing individuals and communities who have successfully made a difference. By highlighting grassroots movements, innovative solutions, and success stories, documentaries empower viewers to become agents of change themselves. As students of film and media studies, we can harness the power of documentaries to mobilize communities, spark conversations, and drive meaningful social progress.

Conclusion:
In the realm of film and media studies, understanding the impact of documentaries is essential for students seeking to make a difference in the world. Documentaries have the power to shape public opinion, raise awareness, and inspire action. By tapping into the potential of non-fiction media, we can become catalysts for change, utilizing storytelling to drive social progress. As we delve deeper into the world of documentaries, let us recognize the immense power they hold and use it responsibly, ethically, and with the goal of creating a more just and equitable society.

Empowering Students to Create Powerful Social Narratives

In today's fast-paced and interconnected world, the power of storytelling has never been more evident. Stories have the ability to shape and transform societies, and documentary filmmaking is one of the most effective mediums for capturing and sharing these narratives. For students interested in film and media studies, understanding the impact of non-fiction media is crucial. This subchapter aims to empower students to harness the power of documentary filmmaking to create compelling social narratives.

Documentary filmmaking is not just about capturing reality; it is about crafting stories that resonate with audiences and ignite social change. Students in film and media studies have a unique opportunity to explore the depths of human experiences, shed light on important social issues, and challenge the status quo. By understanding the impact of non-fiction media, students can become catalysts for change and create powerful social narratives that inspire and educate.

To begin this journey, students must learn the craft of documentary filmmaking. This includes mastering technical skills such as camera operation, editing, and sound design. However, it also entails honing storytelling techniques such as narrative structure, character development, and thematic exploration. By understanding these elements, students can effectively communicate their intended messages and engage audiences on a deeper level.

Furthermore, students must develop a critical eye for analyzing existing documentaries. By studying successful examples of non-fiction media, students can identify the strategies and techniques used to create impactful social narratives. This analysis should extend beyond surface-level observations and delve into the underlying messages, ethical considerations, and cultural implications of each film.

In addition to technical and analytical skills, students must also cultivate empathy and cultural sensitivity. Documentary filmmaking involves interacting with real people and communities, often tackling sensitive topics. By approaching their subjects with empathy and respect, students can capture authentic stories that accurately represent diverse perspectives and experiences.

Finally, students must recognize the importance of collaboration and interdisciplinary approaches. Documentary filmmaking is a multidisciplinary art form that requires collaboration with individuals from various backgrounds, including researchers, activists, and artists. By engaging in interdisciplinary discussions and partnerships, students can broaden their perspectives, access different resources, and create more impactful social narratives.

Empowering students to create powerful social narratives through documentary filmmaking is not just about technical skills; it is about cultivating a deep understanding of the impact of non-fiction media. By honing their craft, analyzing existing documentaries, fostering empathy, and embracing collaboration, students in film and media studies can become agents of change, amplifying marginalized voices, and inspiring social transformation.

Chapter 4: Documentary Ethics and Media Literacy

Ethical Considerations in Documentary Filmmaking

Documentary filmmaking is an influential medium that has the power to shape opinions, challenge beliefs, and bring about social change. However, with this power comes great responsibility. In the pursuit of capturing reality, documentary filmmakers must navigate a myriad of ethical considerations to ensure that their work is fair, accurate, and respectful. This subchapter explores the ethical considerations that arise in the process of creating a documentary, aimed at students in the field of film and media studies.

One of the primary ethical considerations in documentary filmmaking is the issue of informed consent. Filmmakers must obtain the consent of their subjects before including them in their films. This consent should be fully informed, meaning that the subjects understand the purpose of the film, how their story will be portrayed, and any potential consequences of their participation. It is crucial to respect the autonomy and dignity of the individuals being documented, ensuring that their rights are protected throughout the filmmaking process.

Another important ethical consideration is the balance between truth and storytelling. Documentaries have the power to shape public opinion, and as such, filmmakers must strive to present an accurate representation of reality. However, they must also recognize the inherent subjectivity in storytelling and the limitations of their own perspectives. It is essential to maintain a commitment to truth while acknowledging the potential biases and limitations that may arise.

Furthermore, documentary filmmakers must consider the potential impact of their work on the subjects and communities they depict. Sensitivity and empathy are key in portraying individuals and cultures accurately and respectfully. Filmmakers should avoid perpetuating stereotypes, exploiting vulnerable populations, or causing harm through their portrayals. It is important to engage in dialogue and collaboration with the communities being documented, ensuring that their voices are heard and their stories are represented authentically.

Lastly, ethical considerations extend beyond the production stage to the distribution and reception of documentaries. Filmmakers should be transparent about their intentions, sources of funding, and any potential conflicts of interest. They must also respect the privacy and well-being of their subjects, considering the potential consequences of public exposure.

In conclusion, ethical considerations lie at the heart of documentary filmmaking. As students in the field of film and media studies, it is crucial to understand and navigate these considerations responsibly. By obtaining informed consent, striving for accuracy and fairness, respecting cultural diversity, and being transparent throughout the filmmaking process, students can create documentaries that have a positive impact while upholding the ethical standards of the profession.

Balancing Objectivity and Subjectivity in Non-Fiction Media

In the realm of non-fiction media, the question of objectivity versus subjectivity has always been a topic of great debate. As students delving into the field of film and media studies, it is crucial to understand the importance of striking a delicate balance between these two elements.

Objectivity refers to the presentation of facts and information without bias or personal opinion. It involves presenting a fair and balanced view of a subject matter, allowing the audience to draw their own conclusions. On the other hand, subjectivity involves the filmmaker's personal perspective, emotions, and experiences that shape the narrative of a non-fiction piece.

While objectivity is often seen as the ideal approach in non-fiction media, it is essential to recognize that complete objectivity is nearly impossible to achieve. Filmmakers bring their own backgrounds, beliefs, and values to their work. These aspects inevitably influence their storytelling decisions, making it challenging to create a purely impartial presentation.

Subjectivity, when used appropriately, can enhance the storytelling aspect of non-fiction media. It allows the filmmaker to connect with the audience on a deeper emotional level, making the content more relatable and engaging. However, subjectivity should be handled with caution, as an excessive personal bias can undermine the credibility and integrity of the film.

To strike the right balance, aspiring filmmakers and media students must employ a methodical approach. Firstly, thorough research and fact-checking are essential to ensure accurate and reliable information. This helps build a strong foundation of objectivity from which the film can grow.

Secondly, filmmakers should strive to represent multiple perspectives and voices. By including diverse viewpoints, they can avoid the trap of a single narrative and provide a more comprehensive understanding of the subject matter.

Thirdly, transparency is key. Filmmakers should openly acknowledge their subjective viewpoints and motives, enabling the audience to critically evaluate the content presented. This transparency fosters trust between the filmmaker and the audience, allowing for a more meaningful engagement.

Lastly, ongoing self-reflection is crucial for filmmakers. They must constantly assess their own biases and preconceptions to ensure that they do not unduly influence the final product. By being aware of their own subjectivity, filmmakers can make conscious choices that maintain the integrity of their work.

In conclusion, balancing objectivity and subjectivity in non-fiction media is a challenging but essential task for filmmakers and media students. By combining thorough research, multiple perspectives, transparency, and self-reflection, they can create impactful and thought-provoking content that resonates with audiences while maintaining the utmost credibility and integrity.

Addressing Ethical Challenges in Documentary Production

In the world of film and media studies, documentaries hold a unique position as powerful tools for storytelling and social commentary. These non-fiction films have the ability to shape public opinion, challenge societal norms, and shed light on important issues. However, the production of documentaries also poses ethical challenges that need to be carefully considered.

One of the primary ethical challenges in documentary production is the issue of representation. Filmmakers have a responsibility to accurately and fairly represent the individuals or communities they portray in their films. This means avoiding stereotypes, respecting cultural nuances, and giving voice to marginalized perspectives. It is important for students of film and media studies to understand the potential impact of misrepresentation and the ethical obligations they have as documentary filmmakers.

Another ethical challenge is informed consent. When making a documentary, filmmakers often interact with real people who may be sharing personal or sensitive information. Respecting the autonomy of these individuals and obtaining their informed consent is crucial. Students need to learn how to navigate the delicate balance between capturing authentic stories and protecting the privacy and dignity of their subjects.

Additionally, documentary filmmakers must grapple with the question of intervention. In some situations, filmmakers may be tempted to intervene or stage certain events to enhance the narrative or create a more compelling story. While this can be tempting, it raises ethical concerns about truthfulness and transparency. Students must understand the importance of maintaining the integrity of their films and presenting an unbiased account of the subject matter.

Furthermore, the issue of transparency and disclosure is paramount in documentary production. Students must learn to disclose their intentions as filmmakers to their subjects, as well as to their audience. Transparency in the filmmaking process helps build trust with participants and ensures that the audience understands the nature of the documentary they are viewing.

To address these ethical challenges, students of film and media studies should be encouraged to engage in open discussions and critical reflections on the ethical implications of their work. They should be taught to conduct thorough research, seek diverse perspectives, and consult with experts in the field. By doing so, they can create documentaries that not only captivate audiences but also uphold ethical standards and contribute to positive social change.

In conclusion, the production of documentaries in the field of film and media studies presents unique ethical challenges. From representation to informed consent, intervention to transparency, students must navigate these challenges with sensitivity and integrity. By addressing these ethical concerns head-on, students can harness the power of documentary filmmaking to create impactful, thought-provoking films that inspire positive change in society.

Developing Media Literacy Skills through Documentary Analysis

In today's digital age, where media plays a significant role in our lives, it has become crucial for students to develop media literacy skills. Understanding the impact of non-fiction media is particularly important for students pursuing film and media studies. Documentaries, in particular, offer a unique opportunity to delve into real-world issues and explore the power of storytelling through visual narratives.

The subchapter "Developing Media Literacy Skills through Documentary Analysis" aims to equip students with the necessary tools to critically analyze and interpret documentaries. By doing so, students can gain a deeper understanding of the messages conveyed and the techniques employed by filmmakers.

One of the primary goals of media literacy is to help students become active, discerning consumers of media. By analyzing documentaries, students can learn to identify biases, propaganda, and manipulation techniques often employed in non-fiction media. They can develop the ability to question, challenge, and evaluate the credibility of information presented in documentaries.

Furthermore, documentary analysis allows students to explore the ethical considerations associated with the production and distribution of non-fiction media. They can examine the filmmaker's intentions, the potential impact on subjects, and the cultural, social, and political contexts in which documentaries are created. This critical examination helps students develop a well-rounded perspective and fosters empathy and understanding.

The subchapter will provide students with practical strategies to analyze documentaries effectively. It will delve into the visual and narrative techniques used in documentary filmmaking, such as interviews, archival footage, voice-over narration, and editing. By understanding these techniques, students can decipher the filmmaker's intentions and the impact they seek to achieve.

Moreover, the subchapter will explore various genres of documentaries, such as observational, participatory, expository, and reflexive, and discuss the stylistic choices and storytelling approaches used in each. Students will learn to identify different documentary forms and understand how they shape the audience's perception and engagement.

By developing media literacy skills through documentary analysis, students will not only enhance their understanding of non-fiction media but also sharpen their critical thinking abilities. They will become more aware of the power and influence of media, enabling them to navigate the complex media landscape with confidence.

Ultimately, the subchapter "Developing Media Literacy Skills through Documentary Analysis" empowers students in film and media studies to become informed consumers, responsible producers, and active participants in the media-rich world we live in.

Understanding Media Bias and Manipulation Techniques

In today's fast-paced digital age, where information is readily accessible at our fingertips, it is crucial for students studying film and media studies to develop a critical understanding of media bias and manipulation techniques. The subchapter "Understanding Media Bias and Manipulation Techniques" in the book "The Power of Documentary: Understanding the Impact of Non-Fiction Media on Students" aims to equip students with the necessary tools to navigate the complex world of media and make informed judgments.

Media bias refers to the intentional or unintentional favoritism or prejudice that media outlets exhibit while reporting news or presenting information. It is essential for students to recognize that bias can manifest in various forms, such as political, economic, or cultural biases. By understanding media bias, students can discern the underlying agendas and perspectives that influence media representation and storytelling.

Manipulation techniques are another aspect of media that students must grasp. Media manipulation involves the intentional alteration, distortion, or selection of information to shape public opinion in a particular direction. Techniques like emotional manipulation, misleading statistics, selective editing, and framing are commonly employed by media outlets to influence viewers' perceptions and opinions.

To effectively analyze media bias and manipulation techniques, students should develop critical thinking skills. They need to question the sources of information, evaluate evidence, and assess the credibility and reliability of media outlets. The subchapter will delve into the importance of cross-referencing information from multiple sources, fact-checking, and understanding the potential biases of different media organizations.

Moreover, students will explore case studies and real-world examples to enhance their understanding of media bias and manipulation techniques. They will examine how documentaries, news reports, and social media platforms can shape public opinion and perpetuate certain narratives. By critically analyzing these examples, students will gain a deeper insight into the impact of media bias on society.

Ultimately, the subchapter "Understanding Media Bias and Manipulation Techniques" aims to empower students to become discerning consumers and producers of media content. By equipping them with the knowledge and skills to recognize bias and manipulation, students will be better prepared to navigate the media landscape and contribute to a more informed and democratic society.

Through this subchapter, students will gain a comprehensive understanding of media bias and manipulation techniques, enabling them to critically engage with non-fiction media and make well-informed decisions based on a more nuanced understanding of the information presented to them.

Teaching Students to Critically Evaluate Non-Fiction Media

In today's digital age, where information bombards us from every angle, it has become crucial for students in the field of film and media studies to develop the skill of critically evaluating non-fiction media. Non-fiction media, particularly documentaries, have the power to shape public opinion, influence social change, and provide a deeper understanding of the world around us. As future filmmakers and media professionals, it is essential for students to be able to discern fact from fiction, identify bias, and critically analyze the messages conveyed through these media forms.

This subchapter aims to equip students with the necessary tools to approach non-fiction media with a critical eye. By understanding the impact that these media have on society, students will be better prepared to create their own documentaries and contribute to the field in a responsible and ethical manner.

The first step in teaching students to critically evaluate non-fiction media is to introduce them to the concept of media literacy. By exploring the various techniques used by filmmakers to persuade and manipulate audiences, students can develop a heightened awareness of the power dynamics at play. They will learn to question the motives behind the production, the sources of information, and the credibility of the content presented.

Next, students should be encouraged to analyze the documentary's structure and storytelling techniques. Understanding how filmmakers employ narrative devices such as editing, sound design, and cinematography can help students identify the intended emotional response and evaluate the overall impact of the film. By dissecting the filmmaker's choices and techniques, students can assess the effectiveness and authenticity of the storytelling.

Furthermore, students must be taught to critically evaluate the documentary's sources and evidence. They should be encouraged to fact-check claims made within the film and cross-reference them with reliable sources. By understanding how to assess the credibility of the information presented, students can become informed consumers of non-fiction media and avoid perpetuating misinformation.

Lastly, students should be encouraged to reflect on their own biases and perspectives when engaging with non-fiction media. By acknowledging their own preconceptions and actively seeking out diverse viewpoints, students can develop a more nuanced understanding of complex issues. This self-awareness will enable them to approach non-fiction media with an open mind and critically evaluate multiple perspectives.

In conclusion, teaching students to critically evaluate non-fiction media is an essential skill for those studying film and media studies. By equipping students with the tools to discern fact from fiction, identify bias, analyze storytelling techniques, evaluate sources, and reflect on their own perspectives, they will become more responsible and ethical media practitioners. In an era where the impact of non-fiction media is undeniable, this subchapter will empower students to navigate the complex landscape of media with confidence and critical thinking.

Chapter 5: Integrating Documentaries into the Classroom

Strategies for Incorporating Documentaries in Lesson Plans

As students of film and media studies, you have the unique opportunity to explore the captivating world of documentaries. Documentaries offer a powerful medium to understand and analyze real-life events, people, and issues. They not only entertain but also inform and provoke thought, making them an invaluable tool for learning. In this subchapter, we will discuss effective strategies for incorporating documentaries into your lesson plans, enabling you to harness the full potential of non-fiction media in your studies.

1. Pre-screening Activities: Before watching a documentary, engage in pre-screening activities to provide context and generate interest. These can include reading relevant articles, discussing the topic, or brainstorming questions to guide your viewing experience. This preparation will help you approach the documentary with a critical mindset.

2. Note-taking and Reflection: While watching a documentary, take detailed notes to capture key ideas, important facts, and thought-provoking moments. Afterward, reflect on your viewing experience, considering the documentary's impact, effectiveness, and any personal connections you may have made. Writing a reflection paper or engaging in group discussions can deepen your understanding and critical analysis.

3. Comparative Analysis: Compare and contrast documentaries on similar topics, exploring different perspectives and approaches. This exercise will help you gain a broader understanding of the subject matter and develop a more nuanced view. Consider the filmmakers' choices, biases, and the impact they have on the audience.

4. Cross-curricular Integration: Documentaries can be integrated into various subjects beyond film and media studies. Explore how they relate to history, sociology, environmental studies, or even literature. This interdisciplinary approach will enrich your understanding of the documentary's themes and provide a well-rounded perspective.

5. Filmmaking Projects: Take your learning to the next level by creating your own mini-documentaries or short films. This hands-on experience will deepen your understanding of the filmmaking process and allow you to explore your own storytelling abilities. Experiment with different styles and techniques to develop your unique voice as a filmmaker.

6. Guest Speakers and Q&A Sessions: Invite filmmakers, subject matter experts, or individuals featured in documentaries to share their experiences with your class. This personal interaction can provide valuable insights, deepen your understanding of the subject matter, and inspire further discussion and exploration.

Incorporating documentaries into your lesson plans can transform your learning experience and expand your horizons. By following these strategies, you will develop critical thinking skills, enhance your media literacy, and gain a deeper appreciation for the power of non-fiction media. So, seize the opportunity to explore the world of documentaries and let them guide you on a captivating journey of discovery and understanding.

Selecting Appropriate Documentaries for Different Subjects

In today's media-driven world, documentaries have become a powerful tool for understanding complex subjects. Whether you are a student of film and media studies or simply someone interested in expanding your knowledge, knowing how to select the right documentaries for different subjects is crucial. This subchapter aims to provide you with practical tips to ensure you make informed choices when it comes to documentary viewing.

One of the first steps in selecting an appropriate documentary is understanding the subject matter you wish to explore. Different subjects require different approaches, and it is important to choose documentaries that align with your learning goals. For example, if you are studying history, you might consider documentaries that provide a comprehensive overview of a specific era or event. On the other hand, if you are interested in environmental issues, documentaries that focus on conservation efforts or climate change would be more relevant.

Next, consider the credibility of the filmmaker and the sources used in the documentary. Documentaries are meant to inform and educate, so it is crucial to ensure that the information presented is accurate and unbiased. Look for documentaries created by reputable filmmakers or those that have received critical acclaim. Additionally, check if the documentary incorporates a variety of perspectives and expert opinions to present a balanced view of the subject matter.

Another factor to consider is the intended audience of the documentary. Some documentaries are designed for a general audience, while others target specific age groups or educational levels.

If you are a student, it is advisable to choose documentaries that cater to your level of understanding and provide relevant educational content.

Additionally, the style and format of the documentary should be taken into account. Some documentaries follow a traditional narrative structure, while others employ experimental or observational techniques. Consider your personal preferences and learning style when selecting a documentary. If you enjoy a more immersive experience, opt for documentaries that use creative storytelling methods or incorporate personal narratives.

Finally, take advantage of online platforms and streaming services that offer a wide range of documentaries. These platforms often provide user reviews and recommendations, which can help you make informed decisions. Additionally, many educational institutions and libraries have extensive documentary collections, so make sure to explore these resources.

In conclusion, selecting appropriate documentaries for different subjects is a key aspect of enhancing your understanding and knowledge. By considering the subject matter, credibility of the filmmaker, intended audience, style, and format, you can make informed choices that align with your learning goals. Remember, documentaries have the power to educate, inspire, and create a lasting impact, so choose wisely and enjoy the journey of discovery through non-fiction media.

Creating Engaging Activities and Discussion Prompts

In the world of film and media studies, documentaries hold a unique power to captivate and educate audiences. They provide a window into the real world, shedding light on various social, cultural, and environmental issues. As students in this field, it is essential to not only understand the impact of non-fiction media but also to actively engage with it. This subchapter aims to equip you with strategies for creating engaging activities and discussion prompts that will enhance your learning experience.

One effective way to engage with documentaries is through group discussions. By sharing thoughts, opinions, and interpretations, you can gain a deeper understanding of the subject matter. To facilitate fruitful discussions, consider using open-ended questions that encourage critical thinking. For example, "How did the documentary challenge your preconceived notions about the topic?" or "What ethical considerations did the filmmaker have to address?" These prompts will encourage you to analyze the content and form your own opinions.

Another engaging activity is the creation of a documentary review or critique. This allows you to practice your analytical skills while also honing your ability to communicate your thoughts effectively. Consider the various elements of documentary filmmaking such as cinematography, sound design, and storytelling techniques. By assessing these components, you can develop a well-rounded understanding of the documentary's impact.

Furthermore, interactive activities can provide a hands-on approach to learning. For example, you can organize a documentary screening followed by a role-play activity where students assume the roles of the main characters or stakeholders. This immersive experience allows you to empathize with the individuals portrayed in the film and gain a deeper understanding of their perspectives.

Lastly, incorporating multimedia elements into your activities can enhance engagement. Encourage students to create their own short documentaries or multimedia presentations about a related topic. This not only allows for creativity but also provides an opportunity to apply the concepts learned in class.

In conclusion, creating engaging activities and discussion prompts is crucial for students in the field of film and media studies. By actively engaging with documentaries, you can develop a deeper understanding of the impact of non-fiction media. Group discussions, documentary reviews, interactive activities, and multimedia projects all provide avenues for exploration and learning. Embrace these strategies, and you will unlock the power of documentary to transform your educational experience.

Assessing Student Learning through Documentary Projects

In the world of film and media studies, there is a growing recognition of the power of documentary storytelling. Documentaries have the ability to captivate audiences, spark conversations, and inspire change. They allow us to explore real-world issues and experiences, providing a unique perspective on the world around us. As students in this field, it is crucial that we not only consume documentaries but also understand how to create them effectively.

One way to assess our learning in film and media studies is through documentary projects. These projects provide an opportunity for us to apply our knowledge and skills while also showcasing our creativity and understanding of the medium. Through hands-on experiences, we can delve deeper into the art of documentary filmmaking and gain a deeper understanding of its impact on society.

Assessing our learning through documentary projects allows us to demonstrate our ability to research, plan, and execute a documentary from start to finish. It requires us to critically analyze the subject matter, identify key themes, and develop a compelling narrative. By doing so, we hone our research skills, storytelling abilities, and technical expertise.

Furthermore, documentary projects provide a platform for us to engage with real-world issues that are important to us. Whether it's exploring environmental conservation, social justice, or cultural preservation, documentaries have the power to shed light on these topics and inspire action. As students, our documentary projects allow us to contribute to these conversations and make a meaningful impact.

Assessing our learning through documentary projects also allows for self-reflection and growth. As we navigate the process of creating a documentary, we inevitably encounter challenges, setbacks, and moments of triumph. Through these experiences, we cultivate resilience, adaptability, and problem-solving skills. We learn to collaborate effectively with others, to communicate our ideas clearly, and to meet deadlines. These are all essential skills that will serve us well in our future careers in film and media.

In conclusion, assessing student learning through documentary projects is a valuable and effective way to gauge our understanding of the medium and its impact on society. It provides us with an opportunity to apply our skills, explore real-world issues, and make a meaningful impact. By engaging in these projects, we not only enhance our technical abilities but also develop important life skills that will benefit us throughout our careers. So, let's embrace the power of documentary and showcase our learning through these transformative projects.

Designing Documentary-Based Assignments and Assessments

In the ever-evolving world of film and media studies, documentaries have emerged as powerful tools for both education and entertainment. The immersive nature of documentaries allows students to explore real-life issues, gain a deeper understanding of the world around them, and develop critical thinking skills. As an aspiring filmmaker or media scholar, it is crucial to understand how to design effective documentary-based assignments and assessments that maximize learning outcomes. This subchapter aims to provide you with valuable insights on this subject.

When designing documentary-based assignments, it is important to consider the learning objectives you wish to achieve. Are you aiming to enhance your students' research and analytical skills? Or do you want to encourage them to think critically about societal issues? Tailoring the assignment to your desired outcomes will help guide your design process.

One effective approach is to incorporate a research component into the assignment. Encourage students to delve deep into a specific topic related to the documentary they are studying. This could involve conducting interviews, analyzing primary and secondary sources, or even creating their own mini-documentary. By embarking on this research journey, students will not only deepen their understanding but also develop skills in information gathering, analysis, and synthesis.

Another approach is to challenge students to critically engage with the documentary's content. This can be done through the creation of reflective essays, group discussions, or even mock debates. Encourage students to analyze the film's storytelling techniques, the biases present, and the impact it has on its audience. By engaging in these activities, students will sharpen their critical thinking abilities and learn to question the media they consume.

When it comes to assessments, it is important to provide a variety of options that cater to different learning styles and abilities. Assessments could include written essays, presentations, creative projects, or even collaborative assignments. By offering diverse assessment opportunities, you enable students to showcase their strengths and provide a platform for creativity and self-expression.

Ultimately, designing documentary-based assignments and assessments should be a dynamic and engaging process. It is vital to create a learning environment that encourages exploration, critical thinking, and creativity. By incorporating these elements into your assignments and assessments, you empower students to become active participants in their own learning journey, while also equipping them with the necessary skills to navigate the complex world of film and media studies.

Evaluating Students' Understanding and Analysis Skills

In the dynamic world of film and media studies, understanding and analyzing non-fiction media is crucial for students aiming to thrive in this rapidly evolving industry. Whether you aspire to become a documentary filmmaker, a media critic, or simply a discerning consumer of non-fiction content, honing your understanding and analysis skills is essential. This subchapter explores the various methods and techniques used to evaluate students' comprehension and critical thinking abilities in relation to non-fiction media.

To begin, it is important to acknowledge that understanding and analyzing non-fiction media extends beyond passive consumption. Merely watching a documentary or reading about a film's subject matter is not enough. Instead, students must actively engage with the content, critically examining its themes, techniques, and underlying messages. This subchapter will guide you through the process of evaluating your understanding and analysis skills, helping you become an adept interpreter of non-fiction media.

One effective method for evaluating understanding and analysis skills is through class discussions and debates. Engaging in lively conversations with your peers and instructors can help you gain multiple perspectives on a given documentary, enabling you to develop a well-rounded comprehension of the subject matter. By articulating your thoughts and defending your viewpoints, you not only enhance your own understanding but also foster a collaborative and intellectually stimulating environment.

Another valuable tool for evaluating understanding and analysis skills is the creation of analytical essays and research papers. These assignments encourage students to delve deeper into the subject matter, conducting research and formulating thoughtful arguments. By meticulously analyzing the content, structure, and impact of non-fiction media, you develop a critical eye and strengthen your ability to articulate nuanced interpretations.

Furthermore, engaging in hands-on projects, such as creating your own short documentary or participating in media workshops, allows you to apply your understanding and analysis skills in a practical setting. These experiential learning opportunities foster creativity, collaboration, and critical thinking, while also providing valuable feedback from industry professionals.

Ultimately, evaluating your understanding and analysis skills in relation to non-fiction media is an ongoing process. By actively participating in class discussions, producing analytical essays, and engaging in practical projects, you can continually refine your abilities. The power of documentary lies in its ability to inform, inspire, and challenge societal norms. Through the evaluation of students' understanding and analysis skills, this subchapter aims to empower you to become a discerning and influential participant in the world of non-fiction media.

Chapter 6: The Future of Documentary Education

Emerging Trends in Documentary Filmmaking and Education

In recent years, the world of documentary filmmaking has undergone significant transformations, leading to the emergence of exciting new trends that are shaping the field. These trends are not only revolutionizing the way documentaries are made but also impacting the way they are taught and studied. This subchapter explores some of the most prominent emerging trends in documentary filmmaking and education, catering specifically to students with an interest in film and media studies.

One of the key trends in documentary filmmaking is the rise of interactive and immersive storytelling techniques. Filmmakers are now using cutting-edge technologies such as virtual reality (VR) and augmented reality (AR) to engage audiences in more immersive ways. Students studying documentary filmmaking can now explore these techniques and learn to incorporate them into their own projects, pushing the boundaries of storytelling to new heights.

Another trend in documentary filmmaking is the increasing emphasis on social impact and advocacy. Today's documentaries are not just about informing and entertaining; they are often created with the intention of raising awareness and igniting social change. Students can now learn how to use the power of documentary filmmaking to address pressing social issues, giving them the tools to become agents of change through their work.

Furthermore, the democratization of technology has made documentary filmmaking more accessible than ever before. With the advent of affordable equipment and user-friendly editing software, aspiring filmmakers can now create high-quality documentaries without breaking the bank. This trend has opened doors for students to experiment with their creativity and produce compelling non-fiction media that reflects their unique perspectives.

Additionally, the rise of streaming platforms and online distribution channels has revolutionized the way documentaries are consumed. Documentaries are no longer limited to traditional cinema or television screenings; they can now reach global audiences through online platforms. This trend has created a demand for innovative distribution strategies, as filmmakers must navigate the digital landscape to make their work visible. Students can now explore various online platforms, learn about digital marketing, and strategize how to reach their target audience effectively.

In conclusion, the world of documentary filmmaking is constantly evolving, presenting exciting new opportunities for students studying film and media studies. The emerging trends discussed in this subchapter – interactive storytelling, social impact filmmaking, democratization of technology, and online distribution – are reshaping the landscape of documentary filmmaking and education. By embracing these trends, students can equip themselves with the skills and knowledge needed to make a lasting impact through their non-fiction media projects.

Virtual Reality and Interactive Documentaries in the Classroom

In recent years, the realm of documentary filmmaking has witnessed a remarkable transformation with the advent of virtual reality (VR) and interactive documentaries. These groundbreaking technologies have revolutionized the way documentaries are experienced, allowing viewers to immerse themselves in the subject matter like never before. As students of film and media studies, exploring the potential of these innovations can greatly enhance your understanding of the power of non-fiction media.

Virtual reality offers an entirely new dimension to storytelling. With the help of VR headsets, you can step into the shoes of the filmmaker and become an active participant in the narrative. Imagine standing amidst the bustling streets of a foreign city, witnessing firsthand the struggles and triumphs of its inhabitants. VR allows you to travel to distant locations, historical events, or even enter the microscopic world of cells, all from the comfort of your classroom. This immersive experience provides a deeper connection to the subject matter, making it more engaging and memorable.

Interactive documentaries take this level of engagement even further. These documentaries allow you to interact with the content, making choices that shape the narrative and impact the outcome. By offering multiple perspectives and alternative paths, interactive documentaries challenge you to think critically and make informed decisions. This interactive approach not only enhances your understanding of the subject but also encourages active participation, transforming you from a passive viewer into an active learner.

Integrating VR and interactive documentaries into the classroom can have a transformative impact on your learning experience. By using these technologies, you can explore a wide range of topics and gain a deeper understanding of complex issues. For example, you can virtually visit a rainforest to understand the impact of deforestation or explore a war-torn region to comprehend the consequences of conflict. This hands-on approach to learning not only expands your knowledge but also fosters empathy and a sense of global citizenship.

Moreover, VR and interactive documentaries provide invaluable opportunities for experimentation and creativity. As aspiring filmmakers and media enthusiasts, you can use these tools to create your own immersive documentaries, pushing the boundaries of the medium and exploring innovative storytelling techniques. By experimenting with VR and interactive elements, you can engage your audience in new and exciting ways, leaving a lasting impact on viewers.

In conclusion, virtual reality and interactive documentaries have the power to transform the way we learn and understand the world around us. As students of film and media studies, embracing these technologies can open new doors for exploration, creativity, and critical thinking. So, put on your VR headsets and embark on a journey that will revolutionize your understanding of the impact of non-fiction media.

The Impact of Social Media on Documentary Production and Consumption

In today's digital age, social media has revolutionized the way we communicate, connect, and consume information. This impact is especially evident in the realm of documentary production and consumption. As students and enthusiasts of film and media studies, it is crucial to understand how social media has transformed the landscape of documentary filmmaking.

One of the most significant impacts of social media on documentary production is the democratization of content creation. In the past, making a documentary required substantial financial resources, access to specialized equipment, and distribution channels. However, with the advent of social media platforms such as YouTube, Vimeo, and Instagram, anyone with a camera and a story to tell can create and share their documentary with the world. This has led to a proliferation of diverse voices and perspectives, challenging the dominance of mainstream media and allowing for a more inclusive and democratic documentary landscape.

Moreover, social media has also played a vital role in enhancing the visibility and reach of documentaries. Filmmakers can now promote their films directly to their target audience through various social media platforms. This shift has significantly reduced the reliance on traditional distribution channels, enabling filmmakers to bypass gatekeepers and connect directly with their viewers. As students, this means that we have access to an ever-expanding catalog of documentaries, covering a wide range of topics and perspectives, which can enrich our understanding of the world.

Additionally, social media has facilitated the formation of online communities and discussion forums centered around documentary content. Platforms like Facebook groups, Reddit threads, and Twitter hashtags have become virtual spaces where viewers can engage in meaningful dialogue, share their thoughts, and exchange ideas about documentaries. This interactivity not only enhances the viewing experience but also fosters a sense of community among documentary enthusiasts. Through these online communities, students can connect with like-minded individuals, discover new documentaries, and engage in critical discussions about the impact of non-fiction media.

However, it is important to acknowledge the potential downsides of social media on documentary consumption. The abundance of content available online can lead to information overload, making it challenging to discern between reliable and biased sources. As students, we must develop critical thinking skills and media literacy to evaluate the credibility and authenticity of the documentaries we encounter on social media.

In conclusion, the impact of social media on documentary production and consumption cannot be overstated. It has transformed the way documentaries are created, distributed, and consumed, empowering filmmakers and viewers alike. As students and enthusiasts of film and media studies, we have the opportunity to explore and engage with a vast array of documentaries, while also critically analyzing the information presented. By harnessing the power of social media, we can broaden our understanding of the world and contribute to the ongoing dialogue surrounding non-fiction media.

Empowering Students to Be Active Participants in Documentary Culture

In today's digital age, the power of documentary media cannot be underestimated. Documentaries have the ability to inform, educate, and inspire viewers, shedding light on important social, cultural, and environmental issues. As students in the field of film and media studies, you have the unique opportunity to not only consume documentaries but also actively participate in the creation and dissemination of non-fiction media.

Being an active participant in documentary culture means going beyond being a passive viewer. It involves engaging with the content, critically analyzing its messages, and using your skills to contribute to the field. Here are a few ways you can empower yourself to be an active participant in documentary culture:

1. Develop a critical eye: As students of film and media studies, it is crucial to develop a critical eye when watching documentaries. Analyze the techniques used by filmmakers, the narrative structure, and the impact of the content. By understanding the various elements of documentary filmmaking, you can better appreciate the power and influence of non-fiction media.

2. Conduct research: Dive deeper into the subject matter of the documentaries you watch. Conduct research to gain a broader understanding of the issues presented. Explore academic articles, books, and other documentaries related to the topic. This will enable you to contribute to the ongoing conversation and offer informed perspectives.

3. Engage in discussions: Participate in discussions both in and out of the classroom. Share your thoughts, insights, and questions with classmates, professors, and fellow film enthusiasts. Engaging in conversations about documentaries can lead to a deeper understanding of the medium and its impact on society.

4. Create your own documentaries: Take the leap from being a viewer to being a creator. Utilize the knowledge and skills you have acquired in your film and media studies to produce your own documentaries. This hands-on experience will not only empower you but also provide you with a platform to share your perspectives and stories with the world.

5. Utilize digital platforms: In today's digital era, there are numerous platforms available to showcase your work. From social media to online film festivals, these platforms can help you reach a wider audience and contribute to the growing documentary culture. Embrace these opportunities to share your documentaries and engage with other filmmakers and viewers.

By actively participating in documentary culture, you have the potential to make a significant impact. Whether it is through analyzing, researching, discussing, or creating, your involvement in non-fiction media can shape public opinion, raise awareness, and inspire change. Embrace the power of documentaries and let your voice be heard in the dynamic world of non-fiction media.

Encouraging Student Filmmaking and Storytelling

In today's digital age, where media consumption is at an all-time high, there has never been a better time for students to explore the world of filmmaking and storytelling. The power of documentary filmmaking, in particular, cannot be underestimated, as it has the ability to captivate audiences, provoke thought, and inspire change. This subchapter aims to provide students, especially those interested in film and media studies, with the necessary tools and guidance to embark on their own documentary filmmaking journey.

First and foremost, it is important to emphasize the significance of storytelling in documentary filmmaking. Every great documentary starts with a compelling story that engages the audience from beginning to end. Students should take the time to research and identify stories that resonate with them personally and have the potential to make a meaningful impact on a wider audience. Whether it be a social issue, a personal narrative, or a historical event, the key is to choose a subject that evokes passion and curiosity.

Once a story has been chosen, students should familiarize themselves with the technical aspects of filmmaking. This includes learning about camera operation, lighting, sound recording, and editing techniques. While it may seem overwhelming at first, there are numerous online resources, tutorials, and even film clubs or workshops available to help students develop these skills. It is important to remember that mastery comes with practice, so students should not be discouraged by initial setbacks or challenges.

Collaboration is another crucial aspect of student filmmaking. Finding like-minded individuals who share a passion for storytelling can enhance the creative process and provide valuable support. Forming a team with diverse skill sets, such as cinematography, sound design, and writing, can lead to a more well-rounded and professional final product.

Furthermore, students should not be afraid to seek feedback and critique throughout the filmmaking process. Sharing their work with peers, professors, or even industry professionals can provide valuable insights and help refine their storytelling techniques.

Lastly, students should remember that the purpose of documentary filmmaking extends beyond personal achievement. It is a powerful medium for social change, activism, and giving a voice to marginalized communities. By shedding light on important issues, students have the opportunity to educate, challenge societal norms, and inspire action.

In conclusion, encouraging student filmmaking and storytelling is essential for the growth and development of aspiring filmmakers. By delving into the world of documentary filmmaking, students can harness the power of storytelling to engage, inform, and inspire audiences. With the right skills, passion, and determination, the possibilities are endless. So grab a camera, find a compelling story, and let your creativity take flight. The world is waiting for your unique perspective.

Connecting Students with Documentary Communities and Festivals

As students pursuing film and media studies, it is crucial to connect with documentary communities and festivals to enhance your understanding and appreciation of non-fiction media. In this subchapter, we explore the power of these connections and how they can impact your educational journey.

Documentary communities offer a unique platform for students to engage with like-minded individuals who share a passion for non-fiction storytelling. By becoming a part of these communities, you gain access to a wealth of resources and opportunities. Online forums, social media groups, and local meet-ups are just a few avenues to connect with fellow documentary enthusiasts. Engaging in discussions, sharing ideas, and seeking feedback from experienced professionals can greatly enhance your knowledge and skills.

Attending documentary festivals is another incredible way to immerse yourself in the world of non-fiction media. These festivals bring together filmmakers, industry experts, and audiences, providing a vibrant environment to learn, network, and showcase your own work. By attending screenings and participating in panel discussions, you gain valuable insights into the art of documentary filmmaking. Moreover, festivals often host workshops and masterclasses conducted by renowned filmmakers, offering a chance to learn from the very best in the field.

Through these connections, you also gain access to a wide range of documentaries that may not be readily available in mainstream platforms. Many communities and festivals curate and share lesser-known documentaries that tackle important social, cultural, and political issues. By exploring these films, you broaden your horizons and develop a deeper understanding of the world around you. Moreover, these documentaries often offer alternative perspectives and challenge conventional narratives, encouraging critical thinking and analysis.

Additionally, connecting with documentary communities and festivals can open doors to internships, job opportunities, and collaborations. Many filmmakers and production companies actively seek out young talent through these networks. By showcasing your passion, dedication, and skills, you increase your chances of working on exciting documentary projects or gaining valuable industry experience.

In conclusion, connecting with documentary communities and festivals is a vital aspect of your film and media studies journey. It allows you to engage with fellow enthusiasts, expand your knowledge, and explore the diverse world of non-fiction media. Embrace these connections, attend festivals, and actively participate in communities to unlock the full potential of your educational experience. The power of documentary lies not only in the films themselves but also in the communities that support and celebrate them.

Conclusion: Embracing the Power of Documentary for Student Learning

In today's fast-paced world, where information is readily available at our fingertips, the power of documentary filmmaking cannot be underestimated. From exploring historical events to shedding light on social issues, documentaries have the ability to captivate, educate, and inspire. As students in the field of film and media studies, embracing the power of documentary can greatly enhance your learning experience and broaden your understanding of the world around you.

Documentaries offer a unique perspective that textbooks and lectures often fail to capture. They allow you to see real people, real places, and real stories unfold before your eyes. Through the medium of film, you can witness the struggles, triumphs, and complexities of different cultures, societies, and individuals. This firsthand experience not only deepens your understanding but also fosters empathy and promotes critical thinking.

One of the greatest advantages of documentaries is their ability to engage students on multiple levels. They combine visual elements, narrative storytelling, and factual information to create a powerful and immersive experience. This multidimensional approach not only appeals to different learning styles but also ensures a more comprehensive understanding of the subject matter. Whether you are studying history, social sciences, or environmental issues, documentaries provide a wealth of material to explore and analyze.

Furthermore, documentaries offer a platform for alternative voices and perspectives. They challenge the dominant narratives and encourage critical examination of the status quo. By exposing you to different viewpoints and cultural perspectives, documentaries promote tolerance, cultural awareness, and open-mindedness. This is particularly important in today's globalized society, where understanding and appreciating diversity is crucial.

As students of film and media studies, you have the opportunity to not only consume documentaries but also create your own. This hands-on experience allows you to apply the theoretical knowledge you have gained in your studies and develop your own unique voice as a filmmaker. Through the process of researching, interviewing, and editing, you can actively contribute to the world of non-fiction media and make a positive impact on society.

In conclusion, embracing the power of documentary for student learning is an invaluable asset in the field of film and media studies. Documentaries provide a fresh and engaging approach to learning, fostering empathy, critical thinking, and cultural awareness. By delving into the captivating world of non-fiction media, you not only expand your knowledge but also contribute to a more informed and compassionate society. So, grab your camera, dive into the world of documentaries, and let your voice be heard!